CONTENTS

ABOUT CLAY POTS

Clay pots come in a wide range of sizes, from mini 2" (5cm) pots to extra large 8" (20.5cm) pots and beyond. You can find clay pots at most craft stores, as well as flower nurseries and many mass retailers. Most stores carry the standard flowerpot shape, but be sure to keep an eye out for any unique sizes or shapes that might suit the style of your project.

Clay pot sizes are not always exact, and the measurements listed on the pots can vary by store. Ultimately, the projects in this book can be made in any size you'd like. The measurements listed here are general guidelines to give you an idea of the sizes used in this book. All measurements refer to the approximate diameter of the pot opening. The projects will simply refer to the pots as extra small, small, medium, etc. Extremely tiny pots are given a general numeric size such as ½" (1.5cm).

about 2" (5cm)
Mini

about 2½" (6.5cm)
Extra small

about 3½" (9cm)
Small

about 4" (10cm)
Medium

about 3" (7.5cm)
Small tall

about 4½" (11.5cm)
Large tall

Tip

The "tall" pots are sometimes called "rose" pots in the store. These are great for tall, thin projects.

about 8" (20.5cm)

Extra large

about 6" (15cm)

Large

Clay Pot Saucers

Saucers for clay pots are typically sold separately and come in sizes that coordinate with the pots. These are great for crafting as they can be turned into lids or trays for your pots. Before purchasing, make sure you put your pot and your saucer together to make sure they pair nicely. You don't want to arrive home to find you have a saucer that's too big or too small for your chosen pot.

Clay saucers usually come in diameters that match the opening of their corresponding pot. For example, a large pot with a 6" [15cm]-diameter opening will have a matching 6" [15cm] saucer.

ABOUT PAINT

Clay pots are a perfect canvas for paint. The smooth surface makes the painting process thoroughly enjoyable, and the porous clay helps the paint dry quickly. And the end result is always adorable! There are so many wonderful paint products on the market. Here are a few favorites for clay pots.

Acrylic paint. All-purpose acrylic paints are a must-have for painting clay pots. These paints provide good coverage, blend well, and clean up easily. They are widely available and come in dozens of colors and fun finishes, such as metallic and glitter. Best of all, they are inexpensive.

Spray paint. Spray paint goes on quickly and is perfect for a quick pot project. Work in a well-ventilated area and cover your work surface with newspaper to protect it from overspray. Apply two to three thin coats (to avoid dripping) and allow time for the pot to dry thoroughly after each application.

Chalkboard paint. This is a favorite for any craft project! Create a timeless look with classic matte black, or look for other fun colors for a unique twist. The paint is a breeze to apply and clings to the pot's surface very well. Let the paint dry completely and then have fun personalizing the finished pot with chalk.

Chalk-finish paint. Not to be confused with chalkboard paint, chalk-finish paint comes in a variety of colors and has a matte finish that gives your project a cute, rustic look. This type of paint is now widely available at an affordable price in craft stores.

High-gloss paint. This product has super shine! It goes beyond a regular gloss finish—high-gloss paint will make your average clay pot look like a ceramic piece. If you are going for an extra glamorous look, this is the perfect product.

Paint pens. Once your base paint is applied, get creative and embellish your project with paint pens. They come in a variety of colors and point sizes. Use them to decorate your pots with cute faces, patterns, or labels.

PREP AND PAINT TIPS

Here are some helpful tips and tricks to ensure your success when painting clay pots. Pay particular attention to the pot prep section—a very important step to make sure your paint finish and color come out exactly as you want!

Prepping Your Pot

It is very tempting to just jump in and start painting your pots as soon as you get them, but it really pays to do a little prep work! Prepping your pot won't take long at all, and it will ensure your finish looks the way you intended and lasts over time. Also consider that pots sometimes come with a dusty residue that you'll want to remove for a fresh painting surface. Here are some quick and easy steps to get your pot ready for crafting.

Remove labels. Peel any stickers or price tags off the pot surface.

Sand lightly. Using fine-grit sandpaper, smooth the inside and outside of the pot. Be sure to sand off residue left behind from any stickers.

Wipe down. Wipe the entire surface of your pot with a damp, soft cloth and let it dry.

Prime. For the best results, always prime your pots with a water-based primer before painting. When you prime, your chosen paint color will appear much truer to what you see on the package, the paint will go on smoother, and you won't have to use as much of it.

Tip

Terra-cotta is porous and will absorb moisture, including paint. An unprimed pot will soak up your paint, which can distort the color and requires more coats. So take the time to prime!

Painting Tips

Test your paint. Depending on the color and type of paint you are using, it may look different on the pot than it does in the bottle. Test a small stroke on the bottom of your pot to see the color as it will appear on the pot.

Prime your pots. If you have tested your paint and are not happy with the finished color, prime your pot with a water-based primer and test again. Applying your paint to a primed pot should result in a color that's much truer to that in the paint bottle.

Purchase enough paint. Clay pots are porous and soak up a lot of paint, so if you are painting a large project or several pots in the same color, be sure to purchase extra paint. Two small bottles of acrylic paint (2 fl oz [59 ml]) are typically enough to apply two coats of paint to an extra large pot, but it never hurts to have extra on hand, just in case!

Apply enough coats. Some paints provide enough coverage after one coat, but your finished project will look much more polished if you apply two coats (and even three for light colors). Plus, you can use that second coat to touch up any areas you're not quite happy with after your first pass.

Paint everywhere. For most projects it's not absolutely necessary to paint the bottom or inside of your pot, but why not? Painting every surface of your pot will give your finished project some extra polish. And you will avoid last-minute touch-ups after you finish and realize an area you didn't think would be visible actually is!

Test your brush. Foam brushes are great for painting pots, as they will not leave distinct brush marks behind, but be sure to test a variety of options and use the brush that feels the most comfortable and works for you.

Prop your pot. For hands-free painting, place your pot (upside down) over a can or other appropriately sized item so that you can paint all sides easily. This way, you can paint your pot without having to hold it and can let it dry without touching any surfaces.

Tape it off. Use painter's tape or Frog Tape to cover any areas that you do not wish to be painted.

Protect your finish. After painting your pot (and before adding any embellishments like ribbon or beads), spray on a light coat of clear acrylic finish in matte or gloss, depending on your desired look. Be sure to do this in a well-ventilated area.

TOOLS AND MATERIALS

Crafting with clay pots is so much fun because there are endless ways to decorate, embellish, and assemble them. They really are the most hardworking craft surface available! From scrapbook paper to foam to pom-poms and beyond, you can find inspiration everywhere. And when it comes to tools, you don't need loads of equipment—just a few staple items. Below is an overview of some of the materials, embellishments, and tools we will use in this book.

The basics. You'll need some crafting basics like permanent markers, glue, scissors, toothpicks, a ruler, tracing paper, cotton swabs, paper towels, paper plates, and a hole punch.

Craft foam. This handy material will help bring your pots to life. Use it to create adorable eyes, ears, noses, wings, and more! Use the patterns in this book to trace and cut out shapes, or freehand your own designs.

Stickers. Stickers are a super simple way to embellish your projects. Add star stickers to a Christmas tree or shamrock stickers to a leprechaun. Use letter stickers to spell out a message on a party favor.

Beads and bling. Sometimes you need a few special details to take your pot design to the next level. Look in the jewelry aisle as well as the sticker aisle, where you will find loads of stick-on rhinestones. Look for the ones that come in preset strips, making them very easy to apply. These and other jewelry aisle finds are perfect for adding a little sparkle.

Wooden accessories. Wooden knobs can be used to transform a clay pot into a cute character. You can also find lots of precut shapes to use in place of foam. Turn a wooden heart into wings for an angel or a tiny heart into a duck's bill. All you need is a little paint and some imagination!

Pom-poms and chenille stems. Pom-poms make perfect noses and buttons, while chenille stems can be turned into arms, legs, or antennae.

Ribbon and trim. Use ribbon and other trims like ric-rac to create accents for your projects. Ribbon can be used to make bowties, while ric-rac can be used to simulate a shirt collar or even hair.

Paintbrushes. When it comes to clay pots, foam brushes are the best. The paint goes on smoothly and does not drip or streak. Small liner brushes are great for hand lettering and adding small elements like polka dots.

BASIC TECHNIQUES

Crafting with clay pots is fun and easy! Here are some basic techniques that you can use to transform your pots into adorable characters.

Stackables

1. Paint your pots as desired. Then, generously apply glue to the bottom of your base pot.

2. Add the second pot and press the pots firmly together.

3. Wipe away any excess glue with a damp cloth. Let the glue dry before decorating.

Making Heads

 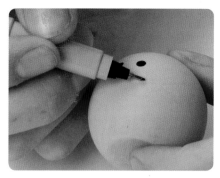 

1. Dot eyes onto a wooden ball with paint, or use a marker. Let it dry.

2. Use a fine-tip permanent marker to draw on the rest of the face.

3. Use decorating chalk or a blush pencil to add blush to the cheeks.

Making Eyes

1. Cut three circles out of foam: two in white for the eyes, and one in a color for the eyelids.

2. Cut the eyelid circle in half. Glue a colored half circle to each white circle.

3. Use a hole punch to punch out pupils from black foam.

4. Glue the pupils to the eyes.

Making Hair

1. Cut 4" (10cm) from a craft feather boa.

2. Apply glue from ear to ear on a wooden ball for the head.

3. Gently press the boa strip in place on the wooden ball.

1. Cut ten pieces of raffia, each 8" (20cm) long.

2. Tie the ten strips together in the center with another piece of raffia.

3. Glue the raffia to the top of a wooden ball for the head, spreading out the individual pieces.

Making Arms

1. Wrap a chenille stem around a pencil to form a tight coil. Repeat with another chenille stem in the same color.

2. Glue the coils to your clay pot character for arms. Let them dry.

3. Bend the arms into position and trim away any excess as needed.

PARTY PALS

Ready to celebrate, these darling little
pals hold treats under their hats.

Materials

- 2 small clay pots
- Craft foam or foam circle stickers in white, black, green, and purple
- Acrylic paint in peach/beige, blue, red, yellow, and orange
- Decorating chalk or blush pencil
- Flat wooden oval or egg shapes
- Cardstock
- Yarn
- Fine-tip black marker
- Paintbrushes
- Glue
- Scissors
- Hole punch
- Tape

1. **Paint the pots.** Paint the base of each pot peach/beige. Paint the rims a different color and decorate them using polka dots, swirls, stripes, or another design of your choice.

2. **Make the faces.** Follow the technique on page 8 to create eyes from the white, black, green, and purple foam. Outline the flat wooden shapes with marker for noses. Glue the eyes and noses onto the pots and draw on the mouths, chins, and eye lines with marker. Add blush to the cheeks.

3. **Make the hats.** Trace the hat pattern onto colored cardstock twice. Cut out the hats and decorate them with polka dots, stripes, swirls, or another pattern. Shape the hats into cones, leaving a small opening at the top, and tape them in place. Make sure the base of the cone will fit inside the opening of your pot.

4. **Make the pom-poms.** Follow the technique for making hair with raffia on page 9 to make a pom-pom for each hat from the yarn. Pull a yarn pom-pom into the point of each hat and tape them in place on the inside of the hats. Fill each pot with candy and cover with the hats.

Too cute! Little partygoers hiding treats under their hats.

Patterns on page 43

LADYBUG

A welcome visitor in any garden, our ladybug welcomes friends with a great big smile.

1. **Paint the pot.** Paint the pot red. Add black polka dots and eyes with black paint or permanent marker. Draw on the mouth with marker. Add blush to the cheeks if desired.
2. **Make the antennae.** Use pliers to curl each end of the wire piece as desired. Glue the antennae in place inside the rim of the pot.
3. **Make the wings.** Trace the wing pattern onto black foam twice. Cut out the wings and glue them to the back of the pot.

Materials

- Small tall clay pot
- Black craft foam
- Acrylic paint in red and black
- Decorating chalk or blush pencil
- 6" (15cm) of 22-gauge gold wire
- Fine-tip black marker
- Paintbrushes
- Glue
- Scissors
- Wire cutters
- Pliers

BUTTERFLY

Flutter by for a tasty treat and a great summer decoration.

1. **Paint the pot.** Paint the pot blue. Add eyes with black paint or permanent marker. Draw on the mouth with marker. Add blush to the cheeks if desired.
2. **Make the antennae.** Use pliers to curl each end of the wire piece as desired. Glue the antennae in place inside the rim of the pot.
3. **Make the wings.** Trace the wing pattern onto purple foam twice. Trace the wing teardrops onto yellow foam twice and onto pink foam twice. Cut out the wing pieces. Outline each teardrop with marker. Glue one teardrop in each color to the purple wings and glue the wings to the back of the pot.

Materials

- Small tall clay pot
- Craft foam in purple, pink, and yellow
- Blue acrylic paint
- Decorating chalk or blush pencil
- Glue
- Scissors
- Fine-tip black marker
- 6" (15cm) of 22-gauge black wire
- Paintbrushes
- Wire cutters
- Pliers

BUMBLEBEE

Stop by my desk for the latest buzzzz and a fun treat.

1. **Paint the pot.** Paint the pot yellow. Add rows of black stripes to the body of the pot with the regular black marker. Draw on the eyes and mouth with the fine-tip marker. Add blush to the cheeks if desired.
2. **Make the antennae.** Use pliers to curl each end of the wire piece as desired. Glue the antennae in place inside the rim of the pot.
3. **Make the wings.** Trace the wing pattern onto white foam twice. Cut out the wings, outline them with marker, and glue them to the back of the pot.

Materials

- Small tall clay pot
- White craft foam
- Yellow acrylic paint
- Decorating chalk or blush pencil
- 6" (15cm) of 22-gauge black wire
- Fine-tip and regular black markers
- Paintbrushes
- Glue
- Scissors
- Wire cutters
- Pliers

Create candy
dishes that are
as cute as a bug
in a rug.

Patterns on page 44

Materials

- Extra small clay pot
- Craft foam in dark green, light green, white, and black
- Green acrylic paint
- Scissors
- Decorating chalk or blush pencil
- 2" (5cm) wooden ball
- Fine-tip black marker
- Paintbrushes
- Glue
- Hole punch

FROG

This prince of a frog will hop right into your heart.

1. **Make the face.** Paint the pot and wooden ball green. Follow the technique on page 8 to create eyes from the white, black, and light green foam. Glue the eyes onto the wooden ball and draw on the mouth. Add blush to the cheeks if desired. Glue the wooden ball to the bottom of the pot.
2. **Make the legs and feet.** Trace the leg pattern onto dark green foam. Also draw four stars onto the foam. Cut out the legs and stars. Glue a star to each end of the legs for feet. Glue the legs onto the back of the pot. Glue the remaining stars to the front of the pot for feet.
3. **Finish.** Punch eight circles from the light green foam using the hole punch. Glue four circles onto each side of the pot for spots.

Materials

- 1 mini clay pot
- 4 extra small clay pots
- 4 small clay pots
- Craft foam in dark green, light green, white, and black
- Green acrylic paint
- Decorating chalk or blush pencil
- Three ⅝" (1.5cm) wooden balls
- Three ¾" (2cm) wooden balls
- Several strands of raffia, 20" (50cm) long
- Fine-tip black marker
- White gel pen
- Paintbrushes
- Glue
- Scissors
- Hole punch

ALLIGATOR

Make this cute critter to decorate a shelf.

1. **Start assembling the pots.** Paint all of the pots green. Knot the raffia strands together several times at one end. Thread an extra small pot, bottom first, onto the raffia followed by a ⅝" (1.5cm) wooden ball. Repeat with two more extra small pots and wooden balls.
2. **Finish assembling the pots.** Thread a small pot, top first, onto the raffia, followed by a ¾" (2cm) wooden ball. Repeat with the remaining pots and wooden balls, ending with a pot. Knot the raffia after this last pot. Glue the mini pot onto the tail end and the remaining extra small pot onto the snout end.
3. **Finish.** Follow the technique on page 8 to create eyes from the white, black, and light green foam. Trace the front and back leg pattern onto dark green foam twice and cut out the legs. Glue the legs and eyes onto the body. Draw on the mouth with marker and the teeth with gel pen. Add blush to the cheeks if desired.

Materials

- 2 small clay saucers
- 1 medium clay saucer
- 4 foam fish
- 4 small foam circle stickers
- Acrylic paint in blue and brown
- Glass bowl that fits inside small saucer (about 3" [7.5cm])
- 8 wiggle eyes
- Thread
- Needle
- Paintbrushes
- Glue

FISH AQUARIUM

This fun fish aquarium is the best catch of the day.

1. **Assemble the aquarium.** Paint one small saucer blue and the remaining saucers brown. Glue the brown small saucer into the medium saucer. Glue the bottom of the glass bowl to the small brown saucer.
2. **Attach the fish.** Glue an eye to each side of each fish. Thread the needle and knot thread onto the top fish fin. Then, push the needle through a foam sticker. Adjust the length of the thread and tie it off so the fish is suspended from the sticker. Attach the sticker to the blue saucer. Repeat with the remaining fish.
3. **Finish.** Glue the blue saucer to the top of the glass bowl, dropping the fish down into the bowl. Fill the bottom saucer with sand or seashells to complete the look.

These characters are a perfect reminder of summer camp and the seashore.

Patterns on pages 44–45

Materials

- 2 extra small clay pots
- Orange craft foam
- Orange acrylic paint
- 2 wiggle eyes
- Paintbrushes
- Glue
- Scissors

GOLDFISH

This friendly fish is happy to be your pet.

1. **Assemble the pots.** Paint both pots orange and glue the rims together. Glue the wiggle eyes to the top of the front pot.
2. **Add the fins.** Trace the tail fin and dorsal fin onto orange craft foam and cut them out. Trace the front fin onto the foam twice and cut them out. Glue the fins in place as shown.

Materials

- 2 extra small clay pots
- Craft foam in blue and white
- Blue acrylic paint
- 2 wiggle eyes
- Paintbrushes
- Glue
- Scissors

SHARK

This shark has lots of pointy teeth, but he's only using them to smile at you.

1. **Assemble the pots.** Paint both pots blue and glue the rims together. Glue the wiggle eyes to the top of the front pot.
2. **Add the fins.** Trace the tail fin and dorsal fin patterns onto blue craft foam and cut them out. Trace the front fin pattern onto the blue foam twice and cut them out. Trace the teeth pattern onto the white foam and cut them out. Glue the fins and teeth in place as shown.

Materials

- 2 extra small clay pots
- Black craft foam
- Acrylic paint in black and white
- Paintbrushes
- Glue
- Scissors

WHALE

Make a miniature version of this ocean giant.

1. **Assemble the pots.** Paint both pots black and glue the rims together. Paint the belly white and add white spots for the eyes.
2. **Add the fins.** Trace the tail fin and dorsal fin patterns onto black craft foam and cut them out. Trace the front fin pattern onto the foam twice and cut them out. Glue the fins in place as shown.

What an ocean of creativity!

Patterns on page 45

PENGUIN

Come in out of the cold with this cute little penguin.

Materials
- Small clay pot
- Black craft foam
- Acrylic paint in black and orange
- Decorating chalk or blush pencil
- White felt
- Flat wooden egg shape
- Black chenille stem
- Fine-tip black marker
- Paintbrushes
- Glue
- Scissors

1. **Prepare the surfaces.** Paint the pot black and the wood shape orange. Trace the body design onto the felt and cut it out.
2. **Make the face.** Add eyes to the felt with paint or marker. Outline the nose and glue it under the eyes. Add blush to the cheeks. Glue the felt belly onto the front of the pot.
3. **Make the wings.** Trace the wing pattern onto the black foam and cut it out. Glue the wings onto the back of the pot. Wrap the chenille stem around the top rim of the pot and twist in the back to secure.

CARDINAL

Tweet, tweet! Make a cheery figure for your favorite bird watcher.

Materials
- Extra small clay pot
- Small clay saucer
- Yellow craft foam stickers in hearts and triangles
- Red acrylic paint
- 1½" (4cm) wooden ball
- Red feather boa cut into two 2½" (6cm) and
- one ½" (1.5cm) pieces
- 1 red chenille stem cut into two 2½" (6cm) pieces
- Spanish moss
- Fine-tip black marker
- Scissors
- Paintbrushes
- Glue

1. **Prepare the surfaces.** Paint the pot and wooden ball red. Glue the pot, top down, into the unpainted saucer. Glue the wooden ball to the pot.
2. **Make the face.** Add eyes with the marker. Add a triangle foam sticker under the eyes for the nose. Add two dots to the nose with the marker. Add two heart foam stickers to the rim of the pot for feet.
3. **Make the wings.** Glue the ½" (1.5cm) boa piece to the top of the head. Wrap each chenille stem around a 2½" (6cm) boa piece for the wings. Glue the wings in place at the shoulders. Glue Spanish moss to the saucer for a nest.

Decorate
your nest
with colorful
characters.

Patterns on page 43

Materials
- Small clay pot
- Small clay saucer
- Green craft foam
- Red acrylic paint
- Brown craft clay
- Paintbrushes
- Glue
- Scissors

APPLE

What an adorable gift to present to your favorite teacher.

1. **Prepare the surfaces.** Paint the pot and saucer red.
2. **Make the leaf and stem.** Cut a large leaf shape from the green craft foam. Glue it to the bottom of the saucer. Make a stem using the clay and glue it on top of the leaf.

Materials
- Medium clay pot
- Large clay saucer
- Acrylic paint in white, teal, and black
- Stone texture finish spray paint
- Glitter
- Large red pom-pom
- Red sparkle chenille stem
- Paintbrushes
- Glue
- Scissors

CUPCAKE

This charming pot looks good enough to eat.

1. **Prepare the surfaces.** Paint the pot teal and add large white polka dots and small black polka dots. Spray the saucer with the stone texture spray paint and then go over it with white acrylic paint.
2. **Make the frosting and cherry.** Cover the saucer with glue and sprinkle it with glitter. Glue the pom-pom to the bottom of the saucer for a cherry. Make a stem by cutting a 2" (5cm) piece from the chenille stem and gluing it to the pom-pom.

Fill these food-inspired pots with delicious treats.

Pattern on page 47

GIRAFFE

This project makes a cute decoration for a nursery.

Materials
- Small clay pot
- Extra small clay pot
- Mini clay pot
- ½" (1.5cm) clay pot
- Brown craft foam
- Acrylic paint in yellow and brown
- 1½" (4cm) wooden ball
- Brown sparkle chenille stem
- Fine-tip black marker
- Paintbrushes
- Glue
- Scissors

1. **Prepare the surfaces.** Paint the small, extra small, and mini pots and the wooden ball yellow. Paint the ½" (1.5cm) pot brown. Glue the small, extra small, and mini pots together in a stack from largest to smallest.
2. **Make the face.** Paint spots on the head with brown paint. Draw on eyes with a marker. Glue the ½" (1.5cm) pot below the eyes for a nose. Add nostrils with the marker.
3. **Add the ears and horns.** Trace the ear pattern onto the craft foam twice and cut them out. Paint the edges of the ears with yellow. Cut two 2" (5cm) pieces from the chenille stem for horns. Fold over one end of each stem for knobs. Glue the ears and horns in place.
4. **Finish.** Paint brown spots randomly over the rest of the body. Glue the head in place on top of the body.

LIGHTHOUSE

This centerpiece is a wonderful way to light your dinner table in the summer.

Materials
- Small clay pot
- Extra small clay pot
- Mini clay pot
- Mini clay saucer
- Acrylic paint in red, white, and black
- Paintbrushes
- Glue

1. **Prepare the surfaces.** Paint the body of each pot red and the rim of each pot white. Paint the saucer black.
2. **Assemble the pots.** Glue the pots together in a stack from largest to smallest. Glue the saucer on top of the stack. Place a tea light in the saucer.

Pattern on page 44

Materials

- Extra small clay pot
- White craft foam
- Pink acrylic paint
- Decorating chalk or blush pencil
- Glitter
- 6 stick-on rhinestones
- 1½" (4cm) wooden ball
- 4" (10cm) pink feather boa piece
- ⅝" (1.5cm)-wide ribbon
- Fine-tip black marker
- Paintbrushes
- Glue
- Scissors

Materials

- Small tall clay pot
- Mini clay pot
- 1" (2.5cm) clay pot
- Green craft foam
- Yellow foam stickers in squares and circles
- Acrylic paint in green and black
- Glue
- Paper towel
- Decorating chalk or blush pencil
- 1¾" (4.5cm) wooden ball
- Chenille stems in orange, green, and black
- Ribbon in black and shamrock
- Fine-tip black marker
- Paintbrushes
- Scissors

Materials

- Small clay pot
- Craft foam in pink, white, and black
- 5 large pink foam hearts
- 2 small pink foam hearts
- 2 small red foam hearts
- Pink acrylic paint
- Pink chenille stem
- Fine-tip black marker
- Paintbrushes
- Glue
- Scissors
- Hole punch

PINK FAIRY

Pretty in pink, this fairy is a wish come true.

1. **Make the face.** Paint the pot pink. Cover the pot with glue and sprinkle it with glitter. Draw the eyes and mouth onto the wooden ball with marker. Add blush to the cheeks. Glue the wooden ball to the bottom of the pot. Glue the boa piece to the top of the head for hair.
2. **Make the wings.** Trace the wing pattern onto white foam and cut it out. Stick three rhinestones onto the end of each wing. Glue the wings to the back of the pot. Make a small bow with the ribbon and glue it on under the chin.

LEPRECHAUN

Share the luck of the leprechaun and his pot of gold.

1. **Make the face.** Paint the tall pot and 1" (2.5cm) pot green. Draw the eyes and mouth onto the wooden ball with marker. Add blush to the cheeks. Glue the wooden ball to the bottom of the tall pot. Coil an orange chenille stem and glue it to the face for a beard.
2. **Make the hat.** Glue the black ribbon around the rim of the 1" (2.5cm) pot. Add a sticker over the ribbon where the ends meet. Cut a circle slightly larger than the opening of the 1" (2.5cm) pot from the green foam and glue it in place over the opening. Glue the hat to the head.
3. **Make the pot.** Paint the mini pot black. Stuff the pot with pieces of a paper towel. Cover the top of the paper towel with foam circle stickers. Make a handle for the pot with a black chenille stem and glue it in place.
4. **Make the arms.** Coil two green chenille stems for the arms and glue them in place. Add a foam shamrock to the end of one arm if desired. Wrap the other arm around the pot handle. Make a small bow with the shamrock-patterned ribbon and glue in place under the chin.

VALENTINE PIG

This special pink pig is all ready to be your Valentine!

1. **Start the face.** Paint the pot pink. Draw on the mouth with marker. Glue a red heart at each end of the mouth. Punch two holes from the black foam and glue them to the top of a large pink heart for the nose.
2. **Finish the face.** Follow the technique on page 8 to create eyes from the white, black, and pink foam. Glue the nose and eyes in place. Glue two small pink hearts upside down on the rim of the pot for ears.
3. **Finish.** Glue four large pink hearts to the bottom of the pot for feet. Coil the chenille stem and glue to the back rim of the pot for a tail.

Create clever and colorful characters for every season.

Patterns on page 48

Materials

- Small tall clay pot
- Light brown craft foam
- Pink foam stickers in circles
- Light brown acrylic paint
- Decorating chalk or blush pencil
- Glue
- Scissors
- Light brown feather boa cut into two 5" (13cm) pieces
- 2 light brown chenille stems
- One large and two small white pom-poms
- Fine-tip black marker
- Paintbrushes

BUNNY

With long angora ears, this charming bunny will hop right into your heart.

1. **Make the face.** Paint the pot light brown. Draw on the eyes with marker. Add a pink foam sticker under the eyes for a nose. Finish the nose by gluing the two small pom-poms in place under the pink sticker. Add blush to the cheeks.
2. **Make the feet.** Trace the foot pattern onto the light brown foam twice. Cut out the feet. Outline each foot with black marker and add three pink circle stickers to the end of each one. Glue the feet in place on the bottom of the pot.
3. **Make the ears.** Wrap a chenille stem around each boa piece for the ears. Glue them in place on the rim of the pot. Bend into shape. Glue the large pom-pom to the back of the pot for a tail.

Materials

- Small tall clay pot
- White acrylic paint
- Decorating chalk or blush pencil
- Black felt
- Gold bell
- Gold cord
- Fine-tip black marker
- Paintbrushes
- Glue
- Scissors
- ⅜" (1cm)-wide blue ribbon
- White curly chenille stems cut into one 1" (2.5cm) piece and one 8" (20cm) piece

LAMB

Baa, baa, white sheep, have you any wool? Yes, sir, yes, sir, three bags full.

1. **Make the face.** Paint the pot white. Draw the eyes and nose onto the rim of the pot with marker. Add blush to the nose and cheeks. Trace the ear pattern onto the black felt twice. Cut out the ears and glue them in place on the pot's rim.
2. **Add the wool.** Glue the 1" (2.5cm) chenille stem to the top of the rim between the ears. Glue the remaining chenille stem around the pot under the rim for wool.
3. **Add the bell.** Make a small bow with the ribbon. Tie the bell onto the bow with the gold cord. Glue the bow in place under the chin.

Materials

- Small tall clay pot
- Acrylic paint in yellow and orange
- Decorating chalk or blush pencil
- 1 large wooden heart
- 2 large wooden stars
- 2 yellow chenille stems
- Fine-tip black marker
- Paintbrushes
- Yellow feather boa cut into two 2" (5cm) pieces
- Glue
- Scissors

CHICK

Fluffy and bright, this chick brings smiles as well as candy.

1. **Prepare the surfaces.** Cut a point off of each star. Paint the stars and heart orange and the pot yellow. Outline the stars and heart with marker. Draw two swirls at the top of the heart with marker.
2. **Make the face.** Draw eyes onto the rim with marker. Add blush to the cheeks. Glue the nose in place under the eyes. Glue the stars to the bottom of the pot for feet.
3. **Make the wings.** Wrap one chenille stem around each boa piece for the wings. Glue them in place at the shoulders.

Springtime is here with these adorable Easter characters.

Patterns on page 48

UNCLE SAM

Uncle Sam wants you to discover the treats hidden under his hat! Show off your patriotic spirit with red, white, and blue pride.

Materials

- Large tall clay pot
- Small tall clay pot
- Small clay saucer
- Craft foam in blue and white
- 3 white foam star stickers
- White feather boa cut into one 7" (18cm) piece
- Scissors
- Paintbrushes
- 2 white foam rectangle stickers
- Acrylic paint in peach/beige, white, and blue
- Decorating chalk or blush pencil
- Small tan pom-pom
- Fine-tip black marker
- Red marker
- Glue

1. **Prepare the surfaces.** Paint the large pot peach/beige and the saucer blue. Paint the base of the small pot white and add red stripes with marker. Paint the rim of the pot blue. Add three star stickers to the rim of the pot. Glue the bottom of the large pot to the bottom of the saucer.
2. **Make the hat.** Trace the bottom of the small pot onto white foam and cut it out. Glue the foam circle to the bottom of the pot. Cut a circle slightly larger than the opening of the small pot from the blue foam and glue it in place over the opening.
3. **Make the face.** Trace the mustache pattern onto white foam twice and cut it out. Draw eyes onto the pot with marker. Add blush to the cheeks. Glue the mustache in place under the eyes and the tan pom-pom on top of the mustache for a nose. Glue the boa in place under the mustache for a beard. Add the rectangles over the eyes as eyebrows.
4. **Finish.** Fill the large pot with candy and cover with the small pot hat.

BASEBALL

Let's play ball! Entertain your team with these tasty treats.

Materials

- Small clay pot
- Blue craft foam
- White acrylic paint
- Red ric-rac
- Paintbrushes
- Glue
- Scissors

1. **Cut out the letters.** Trace the "play ball" pattern onto the blue foam and cut it out. It might be helpful to use a craft knife to cut out the small areas. You might also be able to find this as a sticker at your local craft store.
2. **Finish.** Paint the pot white. Glue ric-rac around the pot as baseball laces. Glue the letters in place on the rim.

Celebrate America with this patriotic character and the country's favorite pastime!

Patterns on pages 48-49

PLAY BALL

Materials

- Small clay pot
- 2 white foam circle stickers
- 1 purple foam circle sticker
- 2 candy corn foam stickers
- 2 black foam letter "I" stickers
- Glue
- Scissors
- Acrylic paint in pea green and black
- Decorating chalk or blush pencil
- Small green pom-pom
- Black ric-rac
- Fine-tip black marker
- Paintbrushes

Materials

- Small tall clay pot
- Black craft foam
- 2 large yellow foam circle stickers
- 2 small white foam circle stickers
- Scissors
- Purple acrylic paint
- Decorating chalk or blush pencil
- Fine-tip black marker
- White gel pen
- Paintbrushes
- Glue

Materials

- Extra small clay pot
- Small clay pot
- Medium clay pot
- 2 large yellow foam circle stickers
- 2 small yellow foam circle stickers
- 2 small white foam circle stickers
- 2 red foam triangle stickers
- 3 white foam square stickers
- 8 green foam heart stickers
- Orange acrylic paint
- Decorating chalk or blush pencil
- 2 green chenille stems
- Fine-tip black marker
- Paintbrushes
- Glue

FRANKENSTEIN'S MONSTER

Dressed in his best bowtie, this monster is ready to party.

1. **Prepare the surfaces.** Paint the base of the pot pea green and the rim black. Glue the ric-rac around the bottom edge of the pot's rim for hair.
2. **Start the face.** Draw pupils onto the white foam circles with marker for eyes. Stick the eyes onto the pot. Add the letter "I" stickers above the eyes for eyebrows. Glue on the green pom-pom for a nose. Draw on the mouth and stitches with marker. Add blush to the cheeks.
3. **Finish the face.** Add the two candy corn stickers under the mouth as a bowtie. Add the purple sticker as the knot at the center of the bowtie.

VAMPIRE BAT

You won't need any bat sonar to find these sweet treats.

1. **Make the face.** Paint the pot purple. Draw pupils onto the white foam circles. Add the white circles to the yellow circles for eyes. Add the eyes to the pot's rim. Draw on the mouth with marker and the teeth with gel pen. Add blush to the cheeks.
2. **Make the wings.** Trace the wing pattern onto black foam and cut it out. Glue the wings onto the back of the pot.
3. **Finish.** Trace the ear pattern onto black foam twice and cut out the ears. Glue them in place on the top edge of the rim above the eyes.

PUMPKINS

Bring a little whimsy to your fall décor with these stacked pumpkins.

1. **Make the faces.** Paint the small and medium pots orange. Draw pupils onto the small white and small yellow foam circles for eyes. Add the small white circles to the large yellow circles. Add the eyes and triangle noses to the pots. Draw on the mouths. Add blush to the cheeks. Add the square teeth.
2. **Make the vines.** Fold the chenille stems in half and thread them through the hole in the bottom of the small pot. Bend the stems inside the pot to secure. Add two hearts to the end of each stem as leaves. Bend or coil the vines as desired.
3. **Assemble the pots.** Glue the unpainted extra small pot onto the medium pot. Glue the small pot on top.

Get ready for some Halloween fun with these adorable characters. Each one is full of personality and treats!

Patterns on page 49

Materials

- Small tall clay pot
- 1" (2.5cm) clay pot
- ½" (1.5cm) clay pot
- Craft foam in black and green
- Acrylic paint in black and green
- Glue
- Decorating chalk or blush pencil
- 1 ¾" (4.5cm) wooden ball
- Orange raffia
- 2 black chenille stems
- 3" (7.5cm) straw broom
- Fine-tip black marker
- Paintbrushes
- Scissors

Materials

- Small tall clay pot
- 1" (2.5cm) clay pot
- ½" (1.5cm) clay pot
- Paintbrushes
- Glue
- Scissors
- 8 yellow foam star stickers
- Purple acrylic paint
- Decorating chalk or blush pencil
- Glitter
- 1 ¾" (4.5cm) wooden ball
- 2 purple chenille stems
- 1 white chenille stem cut into one 2" (5cm) piece
- Fine-tip black marker
- White feather boa cut into one 1" (2.5cm) piece and one 4" (10cm) piece

Materials

- Two extra small clay pots
- 2 large purple foam circle stickers
- Glue
- Scissors
- 2 small yellow foam circle stickers
- White acrylic paint
- Cheesecloth
- Fine-tip black marker

WITCH

Make a bewitching decoration for your table or desk.

1. **Make the hat.** Paint all of the pots black. Glue the ½" (1.5cm) pot to the 1" (2.5cm) pot. Trace the pattern for the hat brim onto black foam and cut it out. Glue it to the 1" (2.5cm) pot.
2. **Make the face.** Paint the wooden ball green. Draw on the eyes and mouth with marker. Add blush to the cheeks. Trace the nose pattern onto green craft foam and cut it out. Glue the nose in place.
3. **Assemble the head.** Follow the technique on page 9 to make hair using the orange raffia. Glue the hair to the top of the head. Glue the head to the tall pot, and glue the hat on top of the head.
4. **Make the arms.** Coil the black chenille stems and glue them to the shoulders as arms. Wrap the end of each arm around the broom.

WIZARD

Make some magic with this star-studded wizard.

1. **Make the hat.** Paint all of the pots purple. Glue the ½" (1.5cm) pot to the 1" (2.5cm) pot. Add two stars to the hat.
2. **Make the face.** Draw the eyes and mouth onto the wooden ball with marker. Add blush to the cheeks. Glue the 1" (2.5cm) boa piece to the chin for a beard. Glue the remaining boa piece to the top of the head for hair. Glue the head to the tall pot, and glue the hat on top of the head.
3. **Make the arms and wand.** Coil the purple chenille stems and glue them to the shoulders as arms. Add three stars to the tall pot. Cover the remaining stars with glue and sprinkle with glitter. Add two stars to one end of the white chenille stem for a wand. Wrap one of the arms around the wand. Add the remaining star to the other arm.

MUMMY

Wrap up some fun with this simple mummy.

1. **Assemble the pots.** Paint the pots white and glue the bottoms together.
2. **Make the face.** Draw pupils onto the yellow foam circles. Add the yellow circles to the purple circles for eyes. Add the eyes below the pot's rim.
3. **Make the wraps.** Cut strips of cheesecloth and glue them around the pots, being sure not to cover the eyes.

These make perfect favors for a Halloween party.

Patterns on page 46

Materials

- Scissors
- Small tall clay pot
- 2 large red foam circles
- 2 large yellow foam circles
- Small foam circle stickers in red, blue, and green
- Acrylic paint in yellow and white
- Decorating chalk or blush pencil
- 1¾" (4.5cm) wooden ball
- Orange feather boa cut into two 1" (2.5cm) pieces
- 2 red chenille stems
- 1 white chenille stem
- 2 large blue pom-poms
- 1 small red pom-pom
- ½" (1.5cm)-wide red ribbon
- Fine-tip black marker
- Paintbrushes
- Glue

CLOWN

Few characters will make you laugh like this cheerful clown.

1. **Make the face.** Paint the pot yellow and the wooden ball white. Draw on the eyes and mouth with marker. Add blush to the cheeks. Glue on the red pom-pom for a nose. Glue a boa piece on each side of the head for hair. Glue the head to the body.
2. **Decorate the body.** Glue the blue pom-poms to the front of the body as buttons. Add the red, green, and blue foam stickers randomly. Make a small bow with the ribbon and glue in place under the chin.
3. **Make the arms and balloons.** Coil the red chenille stems and glue them to the shoulders as arms. Cut the white chenille stem in half. Glue the end of one stem between the two large red circles and the other stem between the two large yellow circles for balloons. Twist the ends of the balloons together and place in the clown's hand.

Materials

- Glue
- Scissors
- Small tall clay pot
- 1 orange foam square sticker
- 1 yellow foam square sticker
- 1 red foam triangle sticker
- Acrylic paint in peach/beige and blue
- 2 blue chenille stems
- Decorating chalk or blush pencil
- 1¾" (4.5cm) wooden ball
- Natural raffia
- ½" (1.5cm)-wide blue plaid ribbon or strip of fabric
- 3" (7.5cm) straw hat
- Fine-tip black marker
- Paintbrushes

SCARECROW

This farmer's helper is too cute to leave in the garden. Display him on a table or shelf.

1. **Make the face.** Paint the pot blue and the wooden ball peach/beige. Draw on the eyes and mouth with marker. Add blush to the cheeks. Add the red triangle for a nose. Follow the technique on page 9 to make hair using the raffia. Glue the hair to the top of the head. Glue the hat on top of the hair. Glue the head to the body.
2. **Decorate the body.** Draw a stitching pattern onto the orange and yellow foam stickers with marker. Add them to the pot for patches. Make a small bow with the ribbon and glue it in place under the chin.
3. **Make the arms.** Coil the blue chenille stems and glue them to the shoulders as arms. Cut small pieces of raffia and wrap the ends of the chenille stems around them as stuffing.

Brighten someone's day by giving them a cute character as a gift.

Patterns on page 47

Materials

- Small clay pot
- 1" (2.5cm) clay pot
- 1 yellow foam square sticker
- Acrylic paint in peach/beige and dark brown
- Decorating chalk or blush pencil
- 1½" (4cm) wooden ball
- White felt
- 8" (20cm) of ⅛" (3mm)-wide black ribbon
- Brown embroidery thread
- Fine-tip black marker
- Paintbrushes
- Glue
- Scissors

Materials

- Small clay pot
- 2 yellow foam triangle stickers
- 1 orange foam square sticker
- Acrylic paint in peach/beige and light brown
- Decorating chalk or blush pencil
- 1½" (4cm) wooden ball
- Tan felt
- Red ric-rac
- Black yarn
- Gold thread
- Yellow feather
- Fine-tip black marker
- Paintbrushes
- Glue
- Scissors

Materials

- Glue
- Large tall clay pot
- 1 large wooden heart
- 2 large wooden stars
- Acrylic paint in orange and brown
- Decorating chalk or blush pencil
- Multi-colored feather boa cut into one 6" (15cm) piece
- Fine-tip black marker
- Paintbrushes
- Scissors

PILGRIM

This smiling pilgrim is ready to celebrate the Thanksgiving season.

1. **Make the face.** Paint the pots dark brown and the wooden ball peach/beige. Draw on the eyes and mouth with marker. Add blush to the cheeks. Follow the technique on page 9 to make hair using the thread. Glue the hair to the top of the head.
2. **Make the hat and collar.** Add the yellow square just below the rim of the 1" (2.5cm) pot and glue the pot to the top of the head. Trace the collar pattern onto white felt and cut it out. Glue the collar in place over the bottom of the small pot.
3. **Glue the head onto the body.** Make a small bow with the ribbon and glue it in place under the chin.

NATIVE AMERICAN

Simple to make, this friendly figure is perfect for your Thanksgiving table.

1. **Make the face.** Paint the pot brown and the wooden ball peach/beige. Draw on the eyes and mouth with marker. Add blush to the cheeks.
2. **Make the hair.** Follow the technique on page 9 to make hair using the yarn. Glue the hair to the top of the head. Make pigtails using the gold thread. Glue the ric-rac around the top of the head for a headband. Glue the feather to the back of the headband. Glue the head to the body.
3. **Decorate the body.** Add the foam stickers to the front of the pot as shown. Cut a ¾" (2cm) strip from the felt long enough to wrap around the rim of the pot. Make small cuts in the felt strip to make a fringe. Glue the fringe in place around the rim of the pot.

TURKEY

Bright feathers make this turkey a festive delight.

1. **Prepare the surfaces.** Cut one point off of each wooden star. Paint the wooden pieces orange and the pot brown. Outline the wooden pieces with marker and add swirls to the heart for a nose.
2. **Assemble the turkey.** Glue the stars to the bottom of the pot for feet. Glue the nose to the rim of the pot. Add eyes above the nose with marker. Add blush to the cheeks.
3. **Add the wings.** Cover the back half of the pot's rim with glue. Press the boa piece in place on the back rim, allowing the ends of the boa to hang down along the sides as wings.

These happy characters are thankful to be a part of your family.

Patterns on page 44

SNOWMAN

Keep this snowman on your table all winter. He will melt your heart!

1. **Prepare the surfaces.** Paint the rim of the pot blue and the body of the pot white. Paint the wooden teardrop orange. Outline the teardrop with marker.
2. **Make the face.** Draw the eyes and mouth on with marker. Add blush to the cheeks. Glue on the orange teardrop for a nose. Wrap the blue chenille stem around the top rim of the pot and twist in the back to secure.
3. **Make the arms.** Cut two 2" (5cm) pieces from one brown chenille stem. Twist each short piece around each end of the remaining chenille stem for hands. Glue the chenille stem to the back of the pot and wrap the ends around for arms.

Materials
- Small clay pot
- 1 small wooden teardrop
- Acrylic paint in orange, blue, and white
- Decorating chalk or blush pencil
- 2 brown chenille stems
- 1 blue chenille stem
- Fine-tip black marker
- Paintbrushes
- Glue
- Scissors

GINGERBREAD MAN

Ready for some Christmas cookies? This gingerbread man will bring a little holiday spice to your home.

1. **Make the face.** Paint the pot and wooden ball brown. Draw on the eyes and mouth with the white paint pen. Add blush to the cheeks. Glue ric-rac around the front of the face for icing. Glue the head to the body.
2. **Decorate the body.** Glue ric-rac around the rim of the pot for icing. Add buttons to the front of the pot with the paint pen. Make a small bow with the holiday ribbon and glue it in place under the chin.
3. **Make the arms and feet.** Trace the arms and feet patterns onto the brown foam and cut them out. Glue ric-rac around the wrists and around the top edges of the feet for icing. Glue the arms and feet to the pot.

Materials
- Extra small clay pot
- Brown craft foam
- Acrylic paint in brown
- Decorating chalk or blush pencil
- 1¾" (4.5cm) wooden ball
- White ric-rac
- 8" (20cm) of ½" (1.3cm)-wide holiday ribbon
- White paint pen
- Paintbrushes
- Glue
- Scissors

ANGEL

This angel can live on your shelf all year round!

1. **Make the face.** Paint the pot white. Draw the eyes and mouth onto the wooden ball with marker. Add blush to the cheeks. Glue the boa piece to the top of the head for hair. Make a 2" (5cm)-diameter loop with the star garland, leaving a 2" (5cm) tail for a halo. Glue the tail of the halo to the back of the head so the loop sits on top of the hair.
2. **Decorate the body.** Glue the doily to the bottom of the pot. Glue the head on top of the doily. Trace the wing pattern onto the white foam and cut it out with scallop-edged scissors. Glue the wings in place on the back of the pot.
3. **Make the arms.** Coil the two chenille stems and glue them to the shoulders for arms. Cut a 6" (15cm) piece from the star garland. Fold the piece in half twice so it is about 1½" (4cm) long. Wrap a hand around each end of the garland piece.

Materials
- Scissors
- Small tall clay pot
- White craft foam
- White acrylic paint
- Decorating chalk or blush pencil
- 1¾" (4.5cm) wooden ball
- 4" (10cm)-diameter cloth doily
- Yellow feather boa cut into one 4" (10cm) piece
- 2 white chenille stems
- Gold star garland
- Fine-tip black marker
- Paintbrushes
- Glue
- Scallop-edged scissors

Snow days bring thoughts of cheer and sweet treats.

Patterns on page 46

CHRISTMAS TREE

This centerpiece sparkles with a bright star.

Materials

- Small clay pot
- Extra small clay pot
- Mini clay pot
- 2 large yellow foam star stickers
- Green acrylic paint
- Small buttons in assorted colors
- Gold ric-rac
- 1 green chenille stem
- Paintbrushes
- Glue
- Scissors

1. **Make the star.** Paint the pots green. Cut a 2" (5cm) piece from the chenille stem. Secure one end of the stem between the two foam star stickers. Push the other end of the stem through the hole in the bottom of the mini pot and bend inside to secure.

2. **Stack and decorate the pots.** Glue the pots together in a stack from largest to smallest. Glue ric-rac around the rim of each pot. Glue the buttons to the pots randomly for Christmas ornaments.

Materials

- Small clay pot
- Craft foam in brown and black
- Brown acrylic paint
- Decorating chalk or blush pencil
- 2 brown chenille stems
- 1 red pom-pom
- Fine-tip black marker
- Paintbrushes
- Glue
- Scissors

Materials

- 4 mini clay pots
- Peach/beige craft foam
- Acrylic paint in peach/beige, red, and green
- Decorating chalk or blush pencil
- Ric-rac in red and green
- 4 gold sequins
- Two 7" (18cm) pieces of holiday ribbon
- Fine-tip black marker
- Regular brown marker
- Paintbrushes
- Glue
- Scissors

Materials

- 2 small clay pots
- White craft foam
- 2 white foam rectangle stickers
- 2 white foam circle stickers
- 1 yellow foam square sticker
- Acrylic paint in peach/beige and red
- Decorating chalk or blush pencil
- 1 tan pom-pom
- White feather boa cut into one 6" (15cm) piece
- 1 black chenille stem
- 1 white chenille stem
- Fine-tip black marker
- Regular red marker
- Paintbrushes
- Glue
- Scissors

REINDEER

Bring a red-nosed reindeer filled with treats as a gift for the host of the next holiday party you attend.

1. **Make the face.** Paint the pot brown. Draw the eyes and mouth on with marker. Add blush to the cheeks. Glue on the pom-pom for a nose.
2. **Make the antlers.** Twist one chenille stem around the center of the other. Wrap the base chenille stem around the top rim of the pot and twist in the back to secure. Bend the ends of the front chenille stem to form antlers.
3. **Make the arms.** Trace the legs pattern onto brown craft foam and the hoof pattern onto black craft foam twice. Cut out the pieces. Glue a hoof to the end of each leg. Glue the legs in place on the back of the pot.

ELVES

Perfect party favors, these hard-working elves serve up a variety of seasonal delights.

1. **Prepare the surfaces.** Paint two pots peach/beige, one pot red, and one pot green. Glue the peach/beige pots onto the colored pots.
2. **Make the faces.** Glue holiday ribbon around the rim of each peach/beige pot. Add lines around the bottom of the rim with the brown marker for hair. Draw on the eyes and mouths with black marker. Add blush to the cheeks. Trace the ear pattern onto the foam four times and cut out the ears. Glue the ears in place on each head.
3. **Decorate the body.** Glue ric-rac around the seams between the pots, using red ric-rac for the green pot and green ric-rac for the red pot. Glue two sequins to the front of each colored pot for buttons.

SANTA

Here comes Santa Claus with holiday treats for all good little boys and girls.

1. **Prepare the surfaces.** Paint one pot and the rim of the second pot red. Paint the body of the second pot peach/beige. Glue the bottoms of the two pots together.
2. **Decorate the body.** Glue the white chenille stem down the front of the red pot, trimming away any excess. Wrap the black chenille stem around the red pot for a belt and twist it in the back to secure. Add the yellow foam square to the front of the black chenille stem for a belt buckle.
3. **Start making the face.** Trace the mustache pattern onto the white foam and cut it out. Draw pupils onto the white foam circles with black marker for eyes. Stick the eyes onto the head. Add the rectangle stickers above the eyes for eyebrows.
4. **Finish making the face.** Draw on the mouth with red marker. Add blush to the cheeks. Glue on the mustache and the pom-pom for a nose. Glue the boa onto the face for a beard.

Ho, ho, ho
and happy
holidays
to all!

Patterns on page 47

IDEA GALLERY

There are so many adorable characters and critters you can make using clay pots. Here are some more ideas based on projects featured in this book. What other fun things can you think of to make?

Try out this variation of the Butterfly project on page 12. Use the same materials, but change the paint color and cut a wing shape similar to the fairy wings on page 48.

Paint some spots on your pot and add a foam nose and ears, and you have a friendly cow. You could also make the spots from foam. Give your cow a bell like you did for the lamb on page 26.

If you made the Valentine Pig on page 24, you might want to make some more friends for him to play with. This elephant can be made with a tall rose pot and gray foam for the head, trunk, and ears.

Bring this lion to life with foam pieces for the head, ears, mane, and feet. Or, you could use a feather boa for an extra fluffy mane.

You can string pots together as you did for the Alligator on page 14 to make a slithering snake. Cut a tongue from red foam and draw stripes onto the body with marker.

Add foam pieces to a clay pot to make a friendly puppy. Use a chenille stem for the tail.

Give this cat a bushy tail by using a feather boa.

Turn the Fish Aquarium from page 14 into a taller design by gluing the fish bowl to a tall rose pot instead of a saucer.

Change the colors of the Cardinal project on page 18 to make a fun bluebird!

Add to your fall décor with this ghostly wind chime. Add the chimes the same way you added the fish to the aquarium on page 14. Purchase some chain in the jewelry aisle of your local craft store and add it to your ghost's hands.

This spider would make an adorable Halloween party favor. Use a clay saucer, chenille stems for legs, and wiggle eyes. Use saucers in different sizes to create a whole spider family!

PATTERNS

Party Pals (page 10)

Party Pal faces

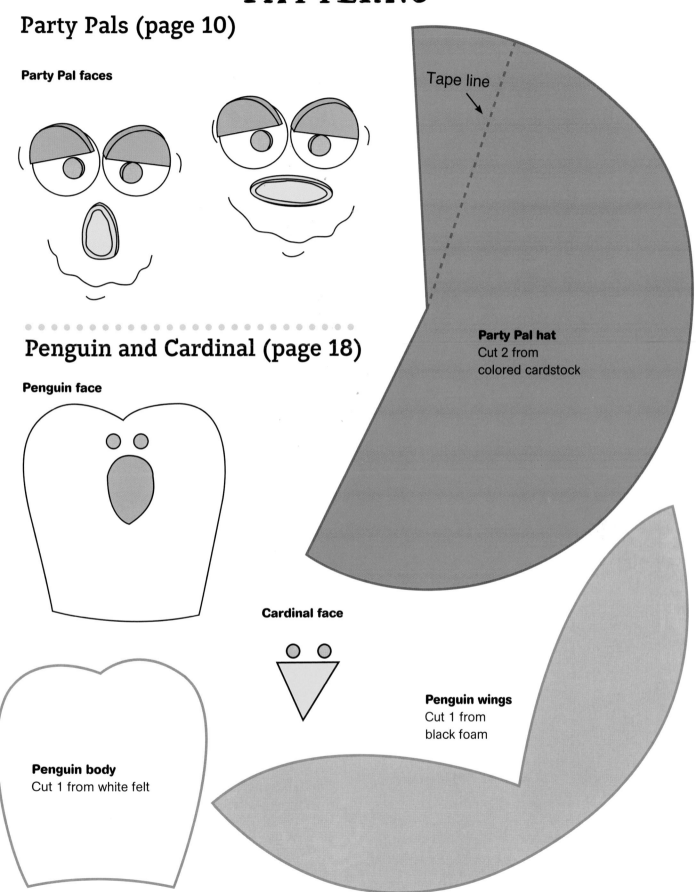

Tape line

Party Pal hat
Cut 2 from
colored cardstock

Penguin and Cardinal (page 18)

Penguin face

Cardinal face

Penguin wings
Cut 1 from
black foam

Penguin body
Cut 1 from white felt

Ladybug, Butterfly, and Bumblebee (page 12)

Ladybug, Butterfly, and Bumblebee face

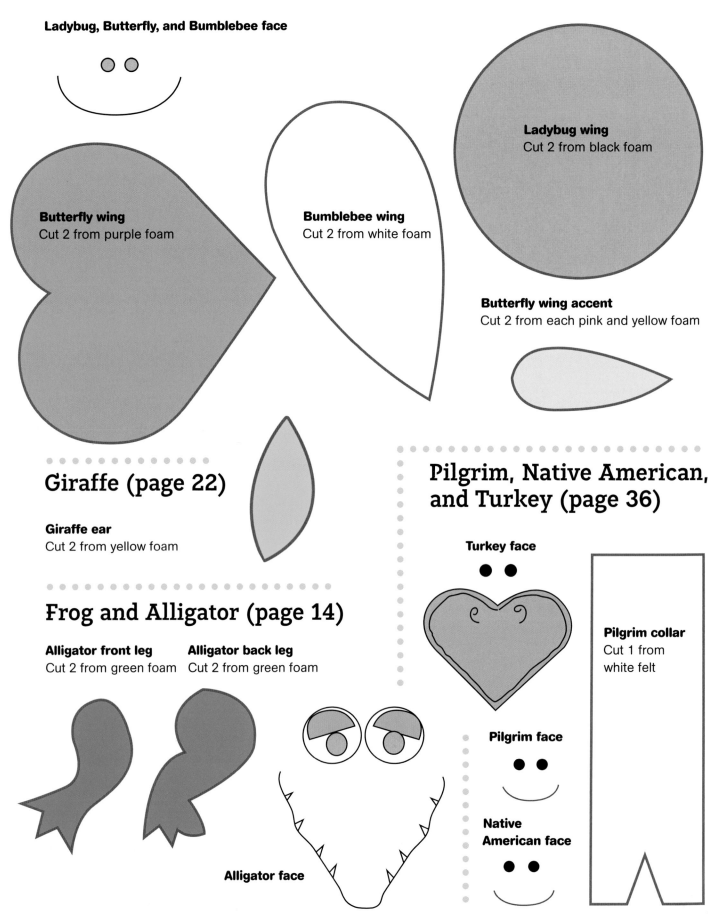

Ladybug wing
Cut 2 from black foam

Butterfly wing
Cut 2 from purple foam

Bumblebee wing
Cut 2 from white foam

Butterfly wing accent
Cut 2 from each pink and yellow foam

Giraffe (page 22)

Giraffe ear
Cut 2 from yellow foam

Pilgrim, Native American, and Turkey (page 36)

Turkey face

Pilgrim collar
Cut 1 from white felt

Frog and Alligator (page 14)

Alligator front leg
Cut 2 from green foam

Alligator back leg
Cut 2 from green foam

Pilgrim face

Native American face

Alligator face

Frog legs
Cut 1 from green foam

Frog face

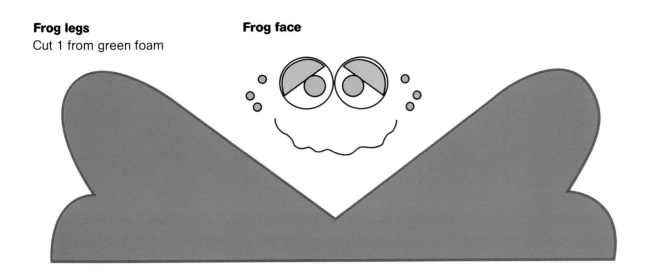

Goldfish, Shark, and Whale (page 16)

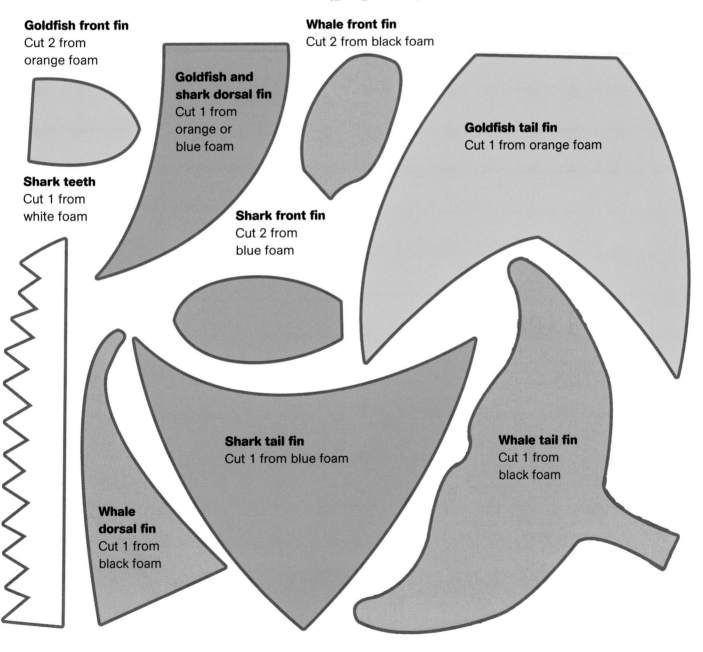

Goldfish front fin
Cut 2 from
orange foam

Whale front fin
Cut 2 from black foam

Goldfish and shark dorsal fin
Cut 1 from
orange or
blue foam

Goldfish tail fin
Cut 1 from orange foam

Shark teeth
Cut 1 from
white foam

Shark front fin
Cut 2 from
blue foam

Shark tail fin
Cut 1 from blue foam

Whale tail fin
Cut 1 from
black foam

Whale dorsal fin
Cut 1 from
black foam

Witch, Wizard, and Mummy (page 32)

Witch face

Witch nose
Cut 1 from green foam

Mummy face

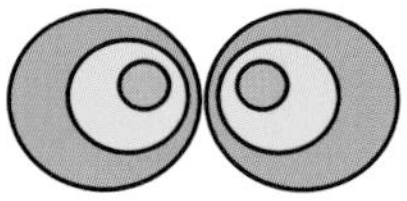

Wizard face

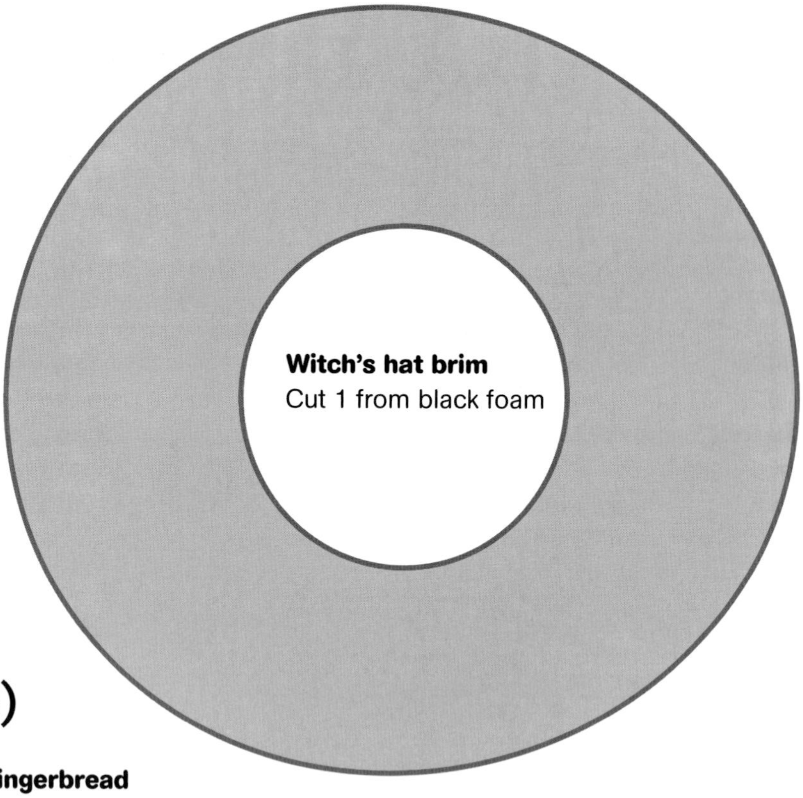

Witch's hat brim
Cut 1 from black foam

Snowman, Gingerbread Man, and Angel (page 38)

Snowman face

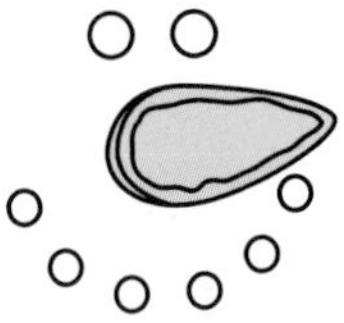

Angel face

Gingerbread Man face

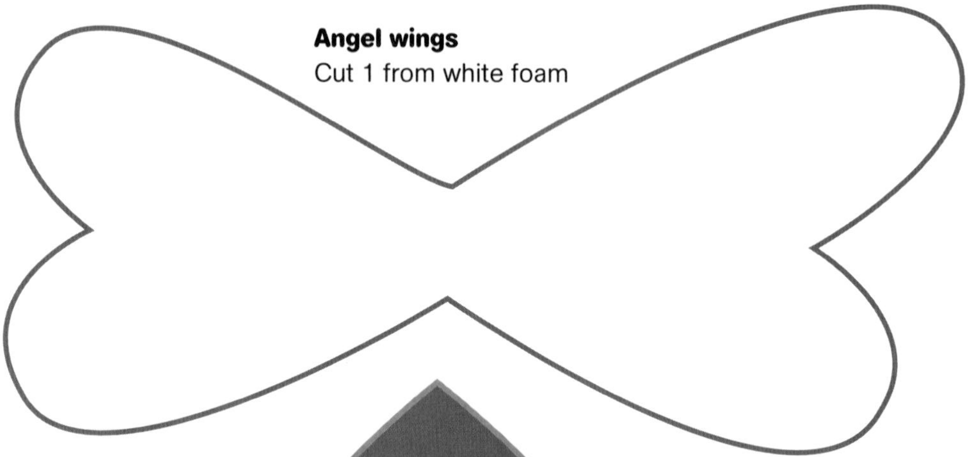

Angel wings
Cut 1 from white foam

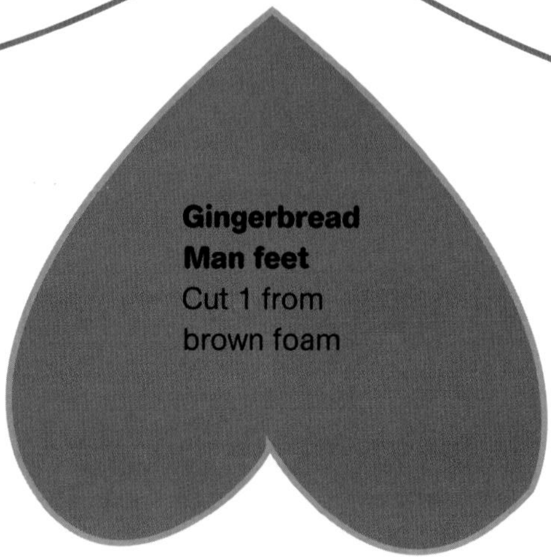

Gingerbread Man arms
Cut 1 from brown foam

Gingerbread Man feet
Cut 1 from brown foam

Reindeer, Elves, and Santa (page 40)

Santa face

Reindeer face

Elf face

Reindeer legs
Cut 1 from brown foam

Santa mustache
Cut 1 from white foam

Elf ear
Cut 4 from peach/
beige foam

Reindeer hoof
Cut 2 from black foam

Apple (page 20)

Apple leaf
Cut 1 from green foam

Clown and Scarecrow
(page 34)

Clown face

Scarecrow face

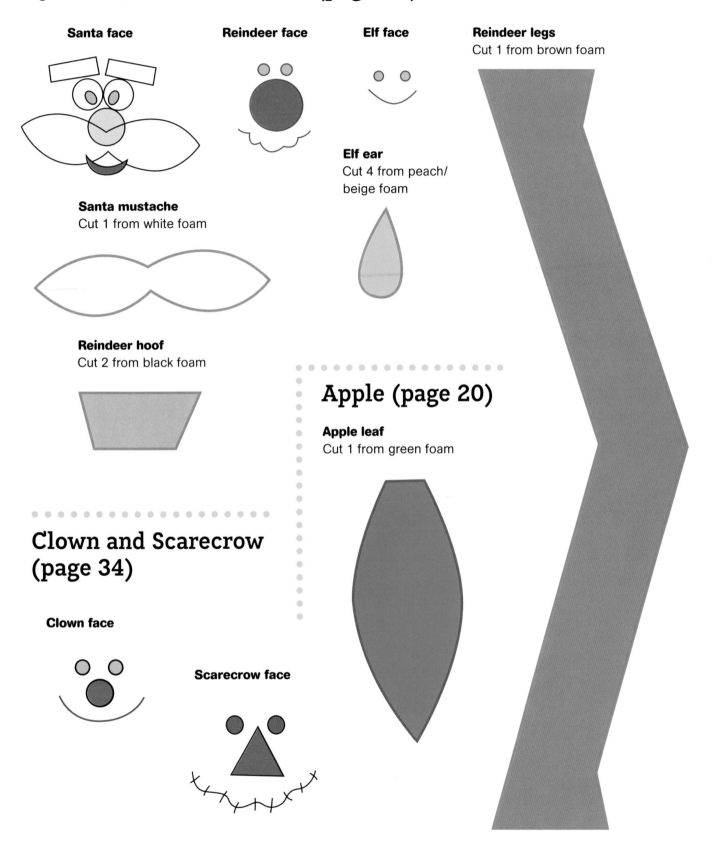

Pink Fairy, Leprechaun, and Valentine Pig (page 24)

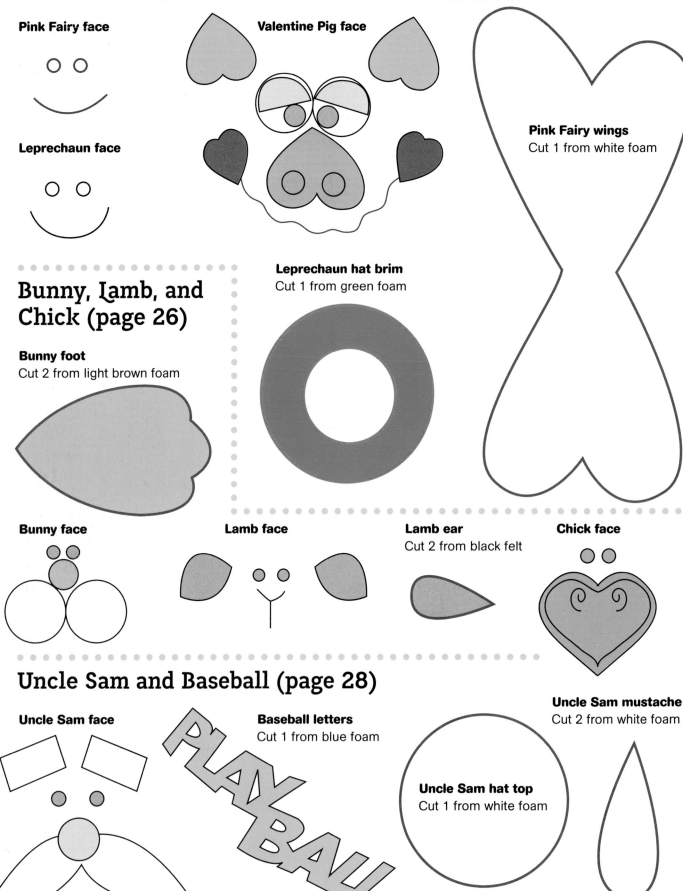

Pink Fairy face

Valentine Pig face

Pink Fairy wings
Cut 1 from white foam

Leprechaun face

Bunny, Lamb, and Chick (page 26)

Leprechaun hat brim
Cut 1 from green foam

Bunny foot
Cut 2 from light brown foam

Bunny face

Lamb face

Lamb ear
Cut 2 from black felt

Chick face

Uncle Sam and Baseball (page 28)

Uncle Sam face

Baseball letters
Cut 1 from blue foam

Uncle Sam mustache
Cut 2 from white foam

Uncle Sam hat top
Cut 1 from white foam